The Gift of Baptism

The
GIFT of
BAPTISM

ROGER HUTCHISON

Illustrated by
CLAIRE WESTWOOD

and sculptor of mountain ranges.

Born under the watchful gaze
of silent animals
and held tightly
in his mother's arms.

Come to earth to teach
God's message of love
and joy.

With water we are baptized, just as John the Baptist baptized Jesus in the River Jordan.

When we receive *the gift of baptism,* we become part of God's loving community, a circle of common good.

Jesus taught people to be kind, caring, and forgiving toward others.

But not everyone listened to his message of love.

Some treated him with disrespect and anger.

Yet he still chose to die on the cross to forgive our sins.

Three days later, the world rejoiced! Like the sweet smoke of incense, he rose again.

I believe in the Holy Spirit,
the fluttering of wings
and flames of
wonder.

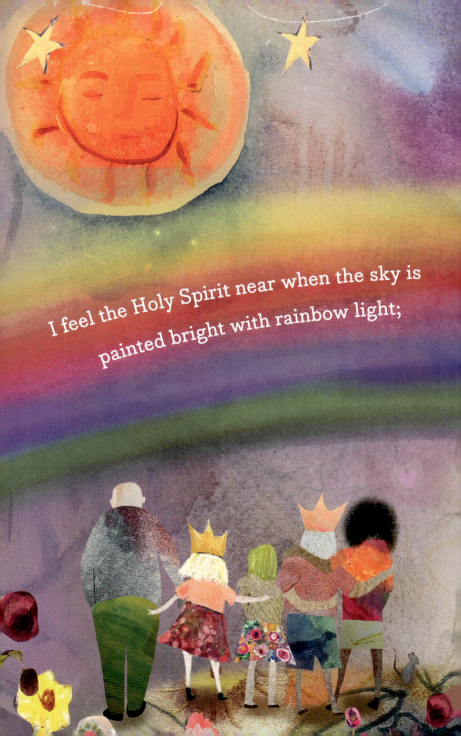

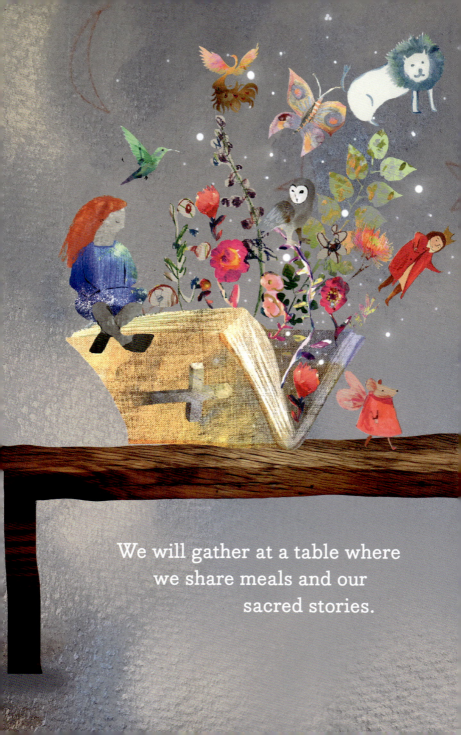

We will gather at a table where we share meals and our sacred stories.

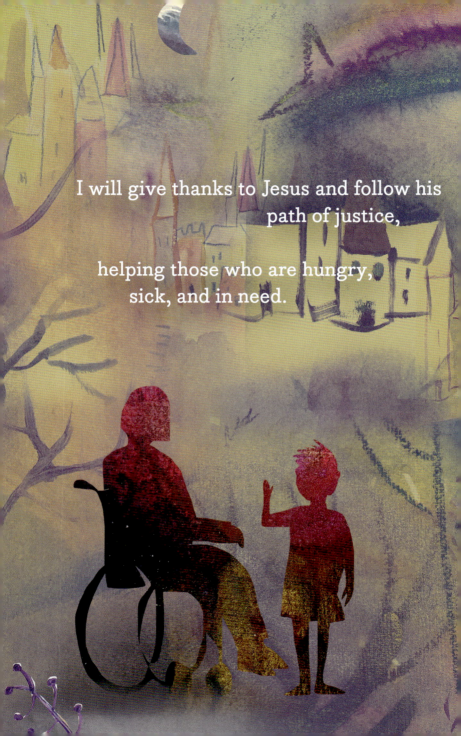

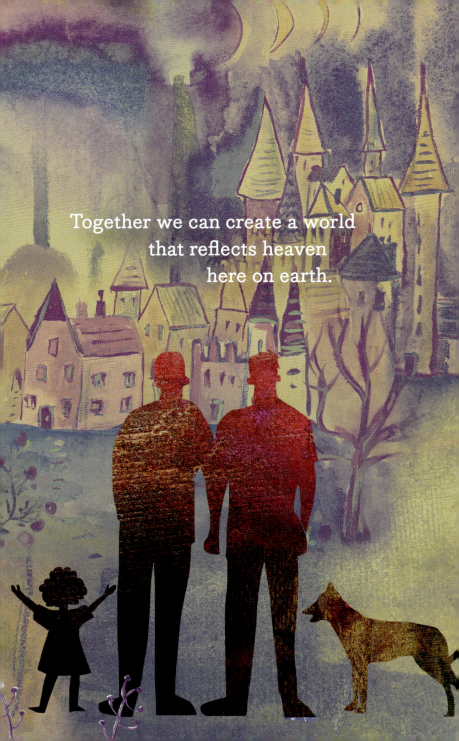

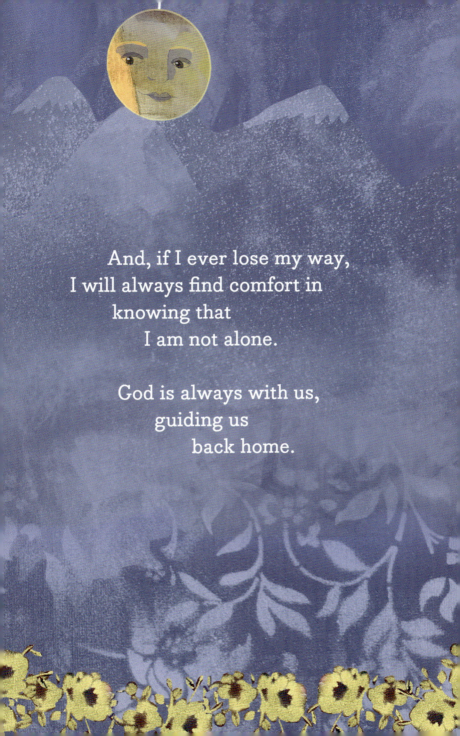

And, if I ever lose my way,
I will always find comfort in
knowing that
I am not alone.

God is always with us,
guiding us
back home.

When we remember our baptism promise, we know that God's love is

I will share the good news of this great love.

I will share it through welcoming hellos,
friendly waves, and warm smiles.
I will share it through my actions,
my words, and my gifts.

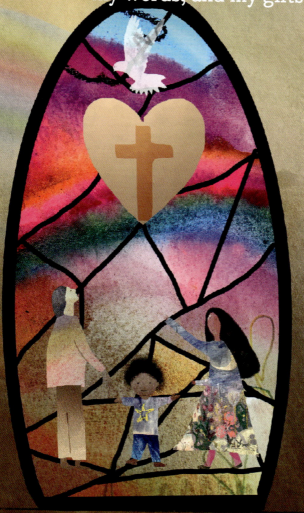

using kind words
and listening with both
my ears and
my heart.

We will go forth in peace and happiness, ready to spread kindness, like wildflower seeds wherever we go.

Closing Prayer:

Dear God, thank you for welcoming me into your family through the gift of my baptism. I am grateful that you have given me a life filled with your loving grace. Bless me with your Holy Spirit so that I may grow in faith, wisdom, and understanding. Help me to be brave and persistent in my journey with you.

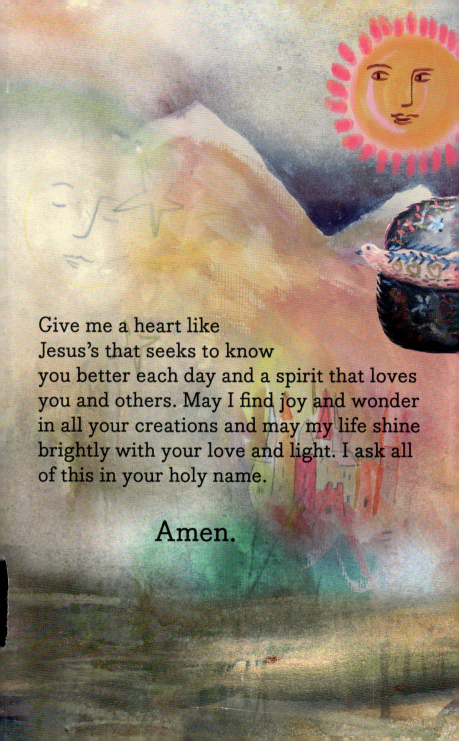

Give me a heart like Jesus's that seeks to know you better each day and a spirit that loves you and others. May I find joy and wonder in all your creations and may my life shine brightly with your love and light. I ask all of this in your holy name.

Amen.

Copyright © 2025 by Roger Hutchison

All rights reserved. No part of this book may be reproduced, stored in a retrieval system, or transmitted in any form or by any means, electronic or mechanical, including photocopying, recording, or otherwise, without the written permission of the publisher.

Morehouse Publishing, 19 East 34th Street, New York, NY 10016

Morehouse Publishing is an imprint of Church Publishing Incorporated.

Illustrations by Claire Westwood
Jacket design by David Baldeosingh Rotstein
Typesetting by Stefan Killen, Red+Company

Library of Congress Cataloging-in-Publication Data

Names: Hutchison, Roger, author. | Westwood, Claire, (Illustrator) illustrator.
Title: The gift of baptism / Roger Hutchison ; illustrated by Claire Westwood.
Description: New York, NY : Morehouse Publishing, [2025] | Audience: Grades K–1
Identifiers: LCCN 2024023862 | ISBN 9781640657540 (hardcover) | ISBN 9781640657564 (ebook)
Subjects: LCSH: Baptism--Juvenile literature.
Classification: LCC BV811.3 .H88 2025 | DDC 234/.161--dc23/eng/20240807
LC record available at https://lccn.loc.gov/2024023862

Printed in Canada